STATUS PENDING

Also by Adrian Blevins

Appalachians Run Amok
Bloodline
Live from the Homesick Jamboree
The Brass Girl Brouhaha
The Man Who Went Out for Cigarettes

and, with co-editor Karen Sayler McElmurray,
Walk Till the Dogs Get Mean, a collection of essays
by new and emerging Appalachian writers.

STATUS PENDING

ADRIAN BLEVINS

FOUR WAY BOOKS
TRIBECA

For Mama—
Phebe Fullerton Cress—
1939 – 2021—
and for my beloved sibs—
Lynn, Shelly, and Mosby—
always there no matter what

This is how we lived.

It was strange.

Elizabeth Strout

Library of Congress Cataloging-in-Publication Data

Names: Blevins, Adrian, 1964- author.
Title: Status pending / Adrian Blevins.
Identifiers: LCCN 2023004551 (print) | LCCN 2023004552 (ebook) | ISBN
9781954245723 (trade paperback) | ISBN 9781954245730 (ebook)
Subjects: LCGFT: Poetry.
Classification: LCC PS3602.L4755 S83 2023 (print) | LCC PS3602.L4755
(ebook) | DDC 811/.6--dc23/eng/20230210
LC record available at https://lccn.loc.gov/2023004551
LC ebook record available at https://lccn.loc.gov/2023004552

This book is manufactured in the United States of America and printed on
acid-free paper.

Four Way Books is a not-for-profit literary press. We are grateful for the assistance
we receive from individual donors, public arts agencies, and private foundations
including the NEA, and the New York State Council on the Arts, a state agency.

We are a proud member of the Community of Literary Magazines and Presses.

CONTENTS

A KIND / OF MIST THAT WAS MORE LIKE SMOG OR RAID OR MSG

NOT / A SPIDER IN THE CORNER OF A JAIL /
IN THE MIDDLE OF THE SAHARA IN LATE / JULY

LOVE POEM FOR LEONARDO DA VINCI

I don't miss the Winn-Dixie or the dopey beauticians
off the old Lee Highway, but my hankering really was a yacht
in high school & I do miss riding it out of the classroom

& into the hall & down the hall & into the parking lot
& through the lot into that plush & sultry biosphere
where there'd be hundreds of hummingbirds flittering around

to sup the red-faced da Vinci feeders hovering like UFOs
on the vessel in the fugitive water-air of my mind in the lab
or math room there where I'd sing to my sweet Leonardo

the Jesus blasphemes my father taught as he took
breath after breath low down inside me down by the river
by the high school there like how the color red is so alive

it throbs if it's blood in your mouth & emits in the brain
what we call the heart when you're just walking down the road
in the fall in Maine at 53 remembering what an insurrectionist

you already were in 1978 in central Virginia in high school
vis-à-vis not wanting the status quo of the space-time continuum
to trap you in that old river valley of church & cakewalks

& doilies & football & the death of deer & date rape

& church & date rape & other good American things

when you & your Leonardo could hop on one of his flying machines

& crank it up   & head   for the love of God   the motherfuck

on out—

ITINERANT GRANNY / HOLED UP A WILY RIDGE

Status, Alas

I began to feel helpless & desperate in a familiar way
in regard to space & time alas & where to put the hands

& feet & how not to talk to strangers & friends
& was raised American & middle class & watched heaps

of TV & got therefore an addictive personality
& a bad biochemistry & anyhow just wanted one day

to buy a few new blankets & quilts & pillows
& sheets. Plus a new skirt & shirt & rug & mug

though outside already was the beefy F-150
waiting to haul me to a cabin up north where there'd be

a tiny roadside store for bread & milk, though also
in the driveway hovered somehow conceptually alas, alas

a mortgage & insurance & car payments & a kid in college
& the need to eat more than bread & milk & an allergist

& a phlebotomist & the primary care physician
& lumberjack & plumber & such & such & such & such

& such. So where to *put* my shopping ache or whatever
as in how to stop it really was the problem like not having

Beebalm to sniff was the problem & the fact of there being
an excellent greenhouse nearby was the problem. & though

a fox I could follow into the woods might help, the problem is
a breeder in Oklahoma selling fox kits for $450 each

not including postage & handling & would I hold mine
& caress it like a child or set it loose is the problem

& how would I feed it or would it feed me
& what would we have to kill & how would we sleep

& can one even grow old in a hole of gnawed bones
& would I even fit & what kind of quilts would there be

& pillows & blankets & sheets?

Exile Status

All my life I've been a stupid little runaway
        & tried therefore to like philosophy
                since beauty pageants

really wouldn't work
        though smoking yes & beer & sex
                a speck, I guess.

But dipping tobacco no
        & pink trucks sorry no
                & no football either

or deer assassination or coons up trees
        or weekends gutting pigs
                & geese. Which is why

I tried with ideas to escape myself
        like ideas are Black-eyed Susans
                or mice. But ideas

are not the Mason jars & homemade jams
        of the Apocalypse
                & ideas are not

the shredded roosters & sourdough starters
  of the Apocalypse & knowing that means
   I'm just an old farmer

milking my cow in the dusk. Or an itinerant granny
  holed up a wily ridge.
   Or a sleepy child

wheeling her little wagon
  down a sleepy road.
   & dusk really is

the main thrill of it as in the point of it
  & the fear of it
   & thus nothing like an idea

though it's duende yes of course
  & what we call the liminal
   since there are bats here too

not to mention my beloved foxes
  curled up in a feral posse
   like a party of furs

& the old & famous
hard rain out there
just drenching us.

IDENTITY STATUS

by *getting lit*
        weekends
                by the river

like Pabst
        opened
                a hole

to some
        boozy netherworld
                where

you could say
        douchebag
                if

you wanted to
        & did
                the drunker

& dumber
        you got?
                So a sot

stripped down

  to nothing

    in the sheds

& shacks

  & fine old water-

    ways

of those old back-

  woods like

    some kind of

porous fume now

  in the old mind

    that really

liked being so sick

  & pissed

    but didn't

but did

  but didn't

    but did?

MEDICAL STATUS

As a matter of fact I did want to get way the fuck down
      to the pith at the beach. Yeah and be like bison

storming some little prefab ranch style thing. But there were
      savage husbands and loopy kids

and we all had laryngitis and the presidents were demons
      and the neighbors were narcs—evildoers basically

with peestraw for hearts. And yeah I thought money
      could fix us (or Frank Lloyd Wright)

here in shitty America where money is your ticket
      if you aren't seen making it. Yeah the mouth

like an oven in the nub of a kiln. O singe and blacken.
      O char and scald! And now just listen to me

coming at you damp and slow like a petty little thing
      with a hole in the heart alone in the dark like a horse cut up.

FALLOUT STATUS

If this is not the best poem of the / century, can it be about the worst
 poem of the / century,
Ammons asks in *Garbage*, & why not let's open that old hatchway
to the sleazy codswallop of the muck of the memory of the backseat
 of that Mustang
in high school out in the boondocks in the Blue Ridge where a
 certain person
lost her limited senses & gave in to love or tried to & found it

O a catastrophe of paper cups / corpse effluvia / wet rust

of amputated trikes / dreg of spit on a black banana

sawdust in a rabbit's mouth / pork crud /

dung heap of toilets / doll heads

& lipstick-licked pink envelopes

& then he squealed like a pig & quaked as he came

& as for the linden trees? As for the tiny frogs that might live in the
 linden trees
& the pelicans if we're talking Florida & the loons here in Maine? As for
the condition of the heart of our certain person post-divorce here in

the Death Empire
in the pre-Apocalypse? Say maybe

the beat-up mannequin of a decapitated wraith in a
    slain Victorian mansion?

                        Say paperclip? / cigarette butt? / some other

                            spook-of-a-thing lying on its side

                        in the sleety afternoon of the gray midwinter

                                of the dump?

OLD BOYFRIEND PRISON STATUS

Something about a child and an inserted object, the mother saying
she and God know he's innocent. Another slumped against a log

in a side yard in Burnt Chimney, a real Virginia place I stir up
for the sound of it and because you should know Southerners can be
    funny

because the comic does distract and who among us can bear to remember
the trillion catastrophes of imprudence floating like apples to bob for

in a tin pan of pale water? The prison one and I would skip school
and drink beer in his car in the parking lot of the Church of the God
    of Prophecy

and fuck up front at dawn. Then we'd talk about how dumb America was
for holding our scorn for math against us, since school in Virginia

in the backwoods back then was like gagging on cocks dipped in corpses
dipped in piss. And anyway at other points in history and in other places

kids like us would be charging the village invaders with our spears
or standing on rocks pounding makeshift drums. But now the prison one

is a person I have to think of as "the prison one" and there are others too
I'd rather not mention—alcoholics drying out in Burnt Chimney

which they also call Reverie and madmen hoarding trash in Troutville
and a journalist on his fourth marriage working the football games

while collecting pennies in a can to pay off a funeral or a Trans Am.
And still even others—schizophrenics downing ludes in honky-tonks

or speeding past the neon to get to the hospital for dialysis or a heart
transplant—broken men I mean delinquents I mean punks and shits

as in actual caged rapists who held me when I was myself a fugitive
en route to these vowel sounds like one can call a downed thing a reverie

though last I heard there are real bricks in Burnt Chimney lying in
    puddles of ash,
is how I want to put it, though *cinder* would also work. *Cinder* and
    tinder and *slag*,

I want to say. *Dross* and *slurry* and *scum. Rat* yeah *yob* yeah *beast*
    yeah *lout.*

CRONE STATUS

however hot I was   & I was a *little* hot
    hot as flapjacks   & a Bic in Atlanta   in the crotch of August
in a graveyard   under Spanish moss   in a sundress
     straddling goneness   dripping lip gloss
       with a cunt like fish sauce   & oh &
with the ghost of a noose   hung in the mugginess
like the tendril of a thing   like a feeling
                     stuck
my croneness is a lot better   it doesn't seal my mouth shut
it wakes me up   & it pisses me off   but it doesn't
     put a pacifier in me   a rampart   a sippy cup

RENEGADE STATUS

Yeah the father was strange
like a smutty goat at the fair
with me in a little knapsack
he'd adorned in pics of nudes
to rile the wannabe Nixon cow-
boys & Nixon bank tellers & sod-
busters & no coal miners per se
but little Nixon ballet dancers
& Nixon climbers of social ladders
& yeah the father was pissed
about Nixon & loud but festive
& drunk I know yet loved
wisteria which looked like grapes
in real life in Italy & on wall-
paper in Southwest Virginia
& loved Mark Twain & Pete Seeger
& washed my hair in Joy detergent
when he couldn't get to the store
& said hamburger was dinosaur
& God was dead & honest I love
all woebegotten things like pigs
& birds midwinter. I love stars,
I love peaches, I love dogwoods,
I love asyndeton but not Nixon

& not war & venal plutocrats
& basic liars & bitches because
the father was strange & drunk
yet bloomed like a fat moon-
flower inside dumbass little me
when I'd run off to mope
as I am doing now to escape saying
how the heart's such a blowtorch
no matter how goofy & late the date.

TRAGEDY STATUS

Are the answers to the questions
    borne of the holes blown through any life
        like the filaments of the quilt
            real backwoodswomen made
                of this lineman's boy's T-shirts

sewn red square to blue & blue square to green
    after he smashed himself to smithereens
        at eighteen? Do I dare even say
            how this lineman had to keep working
                to buy his boy a stone

& himself another truck since the old one's just junk now
    in the dusk? Do I have any right to this story
        of a man weeping beside me
            on a plane? How far into the air
            do light poles go

in Puerto Rico? Can *you* describe the tragedy status
    of sick moms & poor men & dead kids
        & hurricanes? What should I leave out?
            What should I keep in? How relentless
            & perilous really is

                this wind?

Huffy Sicko or / Psycho or Sailor or Whore

Name Status

Out in the country back in the past, Ally made a casserole. Bev thought chicken. Catherine said chicken, yeah, chicken. Dotty put her tomatoes out. Eve and Fiona went for a drive to speak at last of Granny, who Hattie said was daft. Ice is not the name of anybody from out in the country back in the past, though Janice is and Katelyn is and everyone knows at least one old Loretta. Mom named those she was obliged to as best she could. Nan liked Olena's name best, though Olena liked Pepper's and Pepper preferred Quince and Quince, Reece. As for Sam, who knew? And Tex and Urethra? Vicky? Wynona? Not even Xavier would say, though she and poor Yolanda admired their own more urban names most and also Zady's, though only from a distance, as Zady was always wandering off to cry, everyone said, or smoke.

Facebook Status

Ally attended a concert, Bev liked a cat, and Catherine married, at
     long last, that Matt.
Dotty took her driver's test. Eve liked Trump.
Fiona was fired or had some kind of breakdown. Some said the flu.
Granny told everybody to hush. Hattie went to Hattie's church.
Ice decided never to change her name.
Janice called her brave.
Katelyn went to Ireland. Or Katelyn said she did. Katelyn could have
     gone to Walmart. Katelyn could have slept forever in that
     monster's bed.
Loretta posted praying hands, meaning Loretta's praying now,
     waiting for the Apocalypse in her rocker on the porch.
Mom said how much she loved loving the living baby Jesus.
Nan got a beer and Mister Nan got a dog, who got shot.
Olena said nothing. Her status space was status void.
Pepper won the lottery.
Quince broke up with Reece.
Reece posted pics of what everybody said was Quince's pony's little dick.
Sam was searching for a hamster cage and a water bottle and a bike.
Tex was doped up real bad, unless that posting was a joke.
Urethra is not the name of anyone but that comic from LA.
Vicky's child had another little child, a boy.
Wynona liked it. She wanted to undress it.
But Xavier, Xavier said, was blue.

Yolanda too.

Zady said thumbs up to vitamins and little films of fainting goats.

Change of Status

Ally posted the pretty wound of her new tat. Bev pretended to like it. Catherine threatened to divorce her husband and court Dotty or Eve or Fiona, but not Granny and not Hattie and not Ice or Janice or Katelyn or Loretta either and certainly not Mom or Nan though maybe Olena if Pepper would come along with them though not Quince and not Reece. Not Sam. Not Tex. "Court" is not exactly the word Urethra would use for what she thought Catherine was thinking. "Urethra" is obviously Vicky's fake name for comic effect. Vicky knew that, and so did Wynona and Xavier and poor Yolanda. But Zady? You never knew what Zady thought. That Zady acted like she'd had her own mouth sewn shut. She was an enigma wrapped in a whodunit, or however that went. A fiend, a beast, a brute. Our pretty little Satan in a pretty petty petticoat!

STATUS FIELD

Ally wanted cornflowers in the status field. She wanted arrowleaf
   balsamroot.
Bev said that the status field just needed to be got rid of.
Catherine thought that was going too far.
Dotty thought so too.
But cornflowers are weeds! said Bev. And arrowleaf balsamroot
   wouldn't grow anywhere except out west. Plus mice! Plus other
   bugs! Plus rats!
Why not wild bergamot in the status field? Eve asked. Why not aster
   or catchflies?
What even is a catchfly? Fiona wondered. She put her index finger
   into her thinning hair and spun it around like a finger can be a
      spoon. Her eyes got as wide as certain aspects of the International
   Space Station. And more to the point, what even is the status field?
   smart Fiona said out loud.
It has something to do with computers, said Granny, smearing
   something on the counter down.
The status field's got nothing to do with fields! Hattie said. How did
   we even get onto this topic of conversation?
Ice was not even there, so Janice shook her head the way people do.
Katelyn was with her man.
Loretta threw up her hands.
Mom gave the look that said, don't look at me.
Nan had her back turned to everyone. She was doing something to

the stove.

Olena and Pepper googled the status field. It has to do with IBM, they said.

IBM! said Quince. IBM's about as far away from cornflowers as one can get!

Reece threw up her hands.

Sam and Tex and Urethra and Vicky and Wynona and Xavier and Yolanda all did the equivalent of throw up their hands too with a whole hoard of body parts such as Sam's big brown eyes that he rolled.

Of course, Zady liked cursing more than anything in the world, so it came as no surprise to anyone for her to confront the status field with her motherfucks all out like a huffy sicko or psycho or sailor or whore.

TROUBLE STATUS

Ally didn't mind telling Katelyn that all she did was smoke. Which made everything at least two million times worse. But Bev was addicted to Coke. Catherine was anorexic. And Dotty was psychotic! And Eve believed in demons. And therefore not iron supplements. And Fiona loved her gin. And Granny'd taught her how. And Hattie and Ice and Janice bought things every day approximately online. Clothes mostly but also housewares such as crystal glasses and plastic wrap. And towels, Katelyn reminded Ally, and cleaning supplies. And Loretta drove up and down the roads looking for stuff to paint. And Mom's left leg was two inches shorter than her right and Nan and Olena and Pepper and Quince had forgotten how to speak in the seventh grade. They'd forgotten how to care. They just no longer gave the littlest flip. And Reece was loneliness unbounded—loneliness absolute—and Sam was going to smash himself to death on the roads one day. And take Tex maybe with him. And Urethra was the one who needed to change her name since it made you think of pee and Vicky's problem was her very own face in her very own mirror and Wynona's too since this was, after all, the twenty-first century. And weren't Xavier and Yolanda also at risk for everything from hypertension to whatever tumors for which there would be no cure? Not to even mention Zady out there somewhere leaning against a fence post like a dead doll maybe. Like a rotten little birdhouse. Like an urn.

Life Status

Ally told Bev she wanted to die, when she died, asleep. Catherine said, you, Al, asleep? Dotty rolled her eyes and looked out the window. Eve smacked her. Just wake up, Eve said, come on. Fiona had fled to Wyoming for a month, Ally thought, or two. Granny tied the lace of her old shoe. Hattie, somebody said, should be here. Not to even mention Ice. Janice said, however it happens, make it fast. Katelyn thought the worst would be to succumb in childbirth. Loretta wasn't there, either, and neither was Mom. Nan was against the controversial but wondered if "succumb" was really the word to use. She got Ally's broom. She swept and swept. Olena showed everybody her new chemise. Pepper said, I'd rather be at home than all hooked up to a thousand machines. Quince nodded. Reece admitted to two small car wrecks that could've been big. She stared at Sam. Tex sat seeing that. Urethra too. Vicky said, come on, y'all. We're being so morbid. It's not morbid, Wynona said, it's life. Yeah, Xavier and Yolanda said, it's life. Life is life, said Zady, who had just walked through the door. Don't ruin it!

Spit / That Used to Be Paper in the Girl's Diary
with the Word / "Deadfall" Written on It

FLIGHT STATUS

Left for me the ash to heave. Left the lash.
        Left the sieve. Left the chime.

Left the wren. Left the rain. Left an ache.
        Left me dragged

& left me rucking. Left such legroom
        he left me a crypt!

& blew out the stamens okay
        & blew out the sap

until finally I got it that he,
        leaving, left even the milk

our babies spilled
        like a veil across the decades

like he left me counting
        how much airspace

we had to cross
        to get to the end of it

like he left me to say
      how it was to stand over so much slope

to know to be airborne
      which is what I am knowing

plus we're all just vapor
      plus a balefire

& to wake up motherfucker
      & to hew it.

Code Status

But *how* to hew it as in to axe it
        & not end up
                too loud

& /or barbarous & dirtied
        like a schmuck in a park
                in a winter

of rain? How to hoist it
        & it be the halt
                of nothing but

what it's the halt of? Halt
        of the reign of
                the lag between

what was & what's
        not. Halt of man & woman
                as crock

like water under water
        under tillage
                over lean bluestone

& God forbid you should be
   unreliable as a witness
      since already it thins

like ghost spit
   in the back of the neck
      like he was a blowfly

in the eaves of your house.
   Or *you* were
      or the twenty-two years

like pearls on a string
   down a sullied drain
      exceedingly somehow were

& / or the riffle of a leaf
   & / or some fog
      like the blur

of the undo of a rub out
   of the cease of the hum
      of a nothing fade.

RELATIONSHIP STATUS

In this poem he's pitiless. He's worse than a good watch. He's got time
& he's just got to use it out there in the vista that's in my mind in his
    mind

a whirl of strum & sax in a bar where he leans against a pillar in a
    cowboy hat
drinking whiskey delivered on horseback. Plus the walls are mahogany

like it's a Bond movie. &, Adrian, is there smoke? Yes, Adrian, there's
a fuckton of smoke like hot fog off a lake or like smoke smoking

a whole backwoods down though he's not inhaling it since you can't
    inhale
the enthusiasm to wrongly oust people is what I say unless you *can*
    inhale

a ruinous swoop of gust & blow & you *can* inhale a cowboy-Bond
    tsunami
against the whole room & neighborhood & town & city & county &
    galaxy

& cosmos of love. Plus in this poem to mark the various stages of
    grief I guess
you can inhale his spiteful adieu back in that bar that's so dark you

can hardly see

the scowl I mean the cowl he's really under right now like oh, I don't
    know,
he's really just a death moth? A hole in a scythe a cold wind blows
    through?

STATUS UNCERTAIN

In this poem he wasn't even formulated or what-
ever. He was not even spit on his cruel father's lip.

Or in this poem he flew off to Africa six days
before we met. Meaning we did *not* meet—

meaning he's brawling poachers right now in Tanzania
while pulling down the brim of his dumb straw hat.

Or in this poem he actually *is* the poacher stalking gorillas
for their teeth—in this poem he's got a business

selling monkey babes on the streets because in this poem
my heart gets to be a mammoth foghorn

blowing him into every sort of mist because in this poem
he's dead because he wasn't ever born in this poem

because his father never met his mother in West Virginia
in this poem. Or at the very least he's officially condemned

from pulling so many monkey babes off so many
monkey-mama teats. Or he's in a prison in Mexico

for killing a rival drug dealer & he'll be hanged soon
or stabbed or shot & that's sad but I don't know him

so I don't care since I'm not even a ghost to him
in this poem. I am not even the wainscoting

he walked by ten years ago in a bar in London.
I'm not a moth he flicked off a light or a hard-up firefly

he pulled the wings from or a bubble in the cream
in his coffee or a taste bud on his tongue. I am not even

the tiniest cell in his heart where I would have been
had I been there though I am not because in this poem

he wasn't even formulated or devised or what-
ever & thus he could not have left me alone here

to suffer the wail of his dumb adieu—the raw
blubber of it. The daft wreck & waste.

Injury Status

Being left by your husband after twenty-two years
all cloak-and-dagger like my husband left me
is like being hit in the head by the corpse of a fat ballerina
or a snake-handling megawatts church in Needmore,
Virginia like you're the tree of yuck & he's the wave
that makes the wind. Or it's like you're paper—
like you're peed-on paper—like you're spit
that used to be paper in the girl's diary with the word
"deadfall" written on it & "steamroll" & "stymie"
& "drub" & "crush" like you're the runt egg
of a hummingbird & he's a sequoia or you're
an aphid with a respiratory infection & he—he—
he's a paleontologist on the back of a pterodactyl
or you're basically just dying & he's whatever
the opposite of an ambulance is & you're dying
& he's whatever the exact opposite of an ambulance is
such as he's a terrorist or he's strychnine
or a tsunami of swords in the hands of masked rotters
or a poem that doesn't turn like poems should
but just says the thing it says over & over
like being left by your husband of twenty-two years
all cloak-and-dagger like my husband left me
is like being hit in the head by the corpse of a fat ballerina
or a snake-handling megawatts church

in Needmore, Virginia like you're the tree of yuck
& he's the wave that makes the wind.

Refund Status

He called me OUT OF ORDER
& LATE FEE alone in his mind

like a pouch in a purse
where he worked the calculations

like GROSS DOMESTIC PRODUCT
& SUPPLY & DEMAND

in the bank that became his heart
where he's Quid unfortunately

like capitalism taught
& where the quo could not be

babies & could not be
moonflowers. Could not be

seeing foxes out the dawn window
or winter talking walks, the breath

awake—the breath hot—
philodendron trailing a bookcase—

just philodendron just trailing
a simple bookcase

made of felled oak trees
because America is a flub.

A hack. A crime! America,
fuck you for making

despondent bandits of us—
for blinding & hooding

& chaining & gagging us.
You don't seem to know it,

but there are foxes
crossing meadows

out there fast as disco lights.
There are *loons* on your lakes.

Real loons calling right now
their beautifully lamenting

loon hoots or moos or whatever
like they know the only quo

we're ever really going to get
is just a little song of mercy—

just a little mercy song—cooing
into the air like love out there.

Rx Status

Get, little poem, little shoelace
between death & me, the fuck out of bed

& tell the people how dumb marriage is.
How dull & jackass. How un-rife,

but nonstop. Tell them for love you need
no kids for starters & monstrous swaths

like meadows of things like horizons
& moonscapes & skylines to want

& glass buildings & rope ladders
& a faraway beach & hummocks of snow

& fields of breeze-rain in the hair
& on the roof & a drawing pad

like a humongous white canvas of yes
like flecks of lemon on the lips & not—

just *not*—the mouth like a hinge of spit
mouthing the end—holy writ, but counterfeit—of it.

Blabbermouth Status

As for his kiss,
it too was bogus,
the bonkers tongue
all grabby & outback
& oh the mouth
such an O of kvetch
& whine soaked in
such a pit of leaky want
I miss nothing
of him now but
just a few complaints
like how could I
say this & space it
so as to slack
& drift it when
all he did was
just move on
with my friend
the other woman
so lank & gloppy
like a pale forcemeat
of yolk & curd
or a gray ragdoll
against a broken

fence. Why can't I
fathom his need there—
fathom hers—& just
fill my mouth
with mice for once
& just let the story
yawn & gape for him
in spume & blur?

Settlement Status

You take the cranberries & I'll take
the mice. You take the lawn mower—
you take it—& I'll take the rake. You take
the good nozzle & I'll take the grass seed
that I will eat while drinking the wine
that I'll obviously also have to take
as well as the generator that I'll sit on
& pretend is a vacuum. You take
the window, & I'll take the Windex.
You take the light bulbs & I'll take
the sockets & you can take the camera
if I can have that time we first saw
Calvary Cemetery in New York
& Queens when I was like O! O! O!
& you were so very tragically mad
& away & to be fair it really *was*
snowing hard & on your shoulders *was*
the drudgery not to go too fast
on worn tires not to even mention
the desire to play the guitar with me
not nearby plus the fact of how crushing
life was going to be back home in Maine
where so many trees had to be marked
& felled & stacked & chopped & lit

& burned & scooped as ashes out
plus so many nerve-racking shipwrecks
at your work where all the hurt
of all the people of all of poor America
sit to this very day all upon you
sort of snuffing you out, & so you take
the headstone, baby, & I'll take the grave.

ELEGY STATUS

Besides the hatefulness in how he left—
        that mousy getaway that's the worst wrong

spoiling him, an extra rottenness—something tinplate
        & whiptail—sprung up around his fringes

& rooted deep in me like his aura had caught
        the yellow fever. Or some poor child

had drawn a line around him
        like he was just a doodle on the upside

of a dirty cup. Note that he even had an aura
        in my mind during this time

whereas before he'd just been a person.
        This new aura was the aura of a man

whose hair was too dry at the ends in my mind.
        It was the aura of a man

with the bearing of lowlife chainmail
        like he'd drained the druid from him

& poured some ghoul marrow in. O how dare he
    defile my regard for him! O the old sky

of him. The old bloom of him. O the rainwater poise
    & blue-mercy-grace of that lost face!

Marital Status

was a rope across a twilight abyss   (an abscess)
        a small bed too wide   (fog like a slip
              blotched about the bones of a pallid ghost)

palm fronds over a hole   (on Gilligan's Island)
        the polyurethane they spray on mattresses before they attach
the cotton
           (though not the staples they shoot from the gun)

air from the mouth behind his mouth (snake oil & phooey)
      an airfield of silt   (& acid rain)   like it
thought he was there
           & not caper & heist   (not gnaw)

Facebook Status on Why the Marriage Failed

no bareback   I mean horses   no ottoman
or island to put the feet on   not enough boodle
& loot   too much bourbon & gin   not enough
H_2O except in the form of ice   too much
capitalism   barbarism   neutralism   escapism
astigmatism   euphemism   like a greasy lagoon
down the bodyrind of each of us   the five of us
the five of us   the five of us   too much home-
work   & bison   I mean beef   too fast
the minutes   no polecat   no jackdaw
no bullfinch   no wagtail   no linnet
too fast the hours   & years   & years
we needed a smaller bed   less Empire
tent   tent   tinder   fire

RESOLUTION STATUS

1

That place where the husband had carved HALT into the wall?

That grind where you and he had lived, though he didn't hunt though
he did?

Do not forget that lack of sound after the sound of the gun going off.

That swish of the difference between the tree and the rain.

That air between the water and the wave.

That hatchet job, that hole in that bed, the dearth of the loss of that
stalemate.

Like before you were born and once you die in a cesspit undersea.

Like your heart was hooked to a backlog of machetes.

And you were a shovel, a bucket, a backhoe, a spade.

You almost put your ear on the window.

That is, you did.

You felt to yourself that the world was no more than one last guffaw
or wince.

It is hard to say which.

That is, whatever it was that was out there after your husband left.

Bobcat, chipmunk, woodpecker, fox?

Madman? Octopus? Cop?

It wanted you to make a fire.

You really could hear that.

You were the real pair.

You couldn't get enough.

2

You have to remember it to eradicate it.

You were a thing to be collected into a cup to be tossed.

Always was the thing torn off.

And here it was time to come to the senses and think about
something else for once.

Like dead trout, orphans in vestibules, mewing aggregations of
one-eyed dolls on glass shelves in antique stores in the most
rural of counties on the worst days in April in the rain and
the husband out there elsewhere like a wet match.

Like a vellum nut.

Like a suit on the back of a chair during the last bits of a long week of
fast.

Only he's so sleazy you need a loofah and somebody to pump the
well so you can work up a good lather only you are stuck to your
chair in your house on earth like you always were a shoestring in
the dog's mouth.

Old stub in your jaw like a blast.

Old crash in your pectus and each cell's got an eye and each eye's
pulled out a monocle with the whole body looking up through the
nerves for some way out and the heart especially vibrating like it's
the frothing part of an epileptic ship.

O freighter heart   O flotilla heart   O cosmic
belligerency of the ditched heart

Gone husband gone without a word   like nobody   like nothing
Nada nada   zero zero   nil nil   naught.

BEREAVEMENT STATUS

& then you lose your losses—you un-blues your tosses—
     out at the transfer station that's really just a dump

trying to remember what the crying was for & the trying was for,
     tossing the pewter vase he gave you & the sad face

he made you make & this & that old shirt & bowl & plate
     out in Oakland in North America during the Trump Era

in Maine at the dump in Oakland during COVID at the dump
     under a mask with the containers from Wendy's

& the slimy Glad bags & rusted brushes & cables & dial-up phones
     you wouldn't call him on now even if you could

remember the number as somehow you've lost the sense of—
     what was it—something between you two that bound you—

not a clothesline or a wire—something something like a circuit
     or a cord—something—a chilly towline—a thread—a
sword—

A Kind /of Mist That Was More Like Smog or Raid or MSG

Status Quo

1

Status Quo wanted to try a séance—to sit in the dark with the soundly dead. She wanted to have a wolf maybe love her, and for her to love it really back, and for each one to lick the other's face. She imagined him with her and her with him and a leash the color of supple red leather, a mountain they could climb. Status Quo wanted to eat a squid dipped in spiced mayo. Maybe chili peppers and mustard, maybe kale or something more clandestine from the not-fetid waters of maybe 'Nam. She sat wherever she was and thought of her wanting as a kind of mist that was more like smog or Raid or MSG that she wanted to tag like a toe in the morgue so she'd be better prepared next time.

2

Status Quo could not wrap her head around football, so she went to the library to study the vocabulary. On the way she bought a dark blue jersey. She put it on and took off her panties. But then she put them right back on again.

3

Status Quo loved tennis and tennis balls and tennis courts and nets and nets and nets and nets and nets.

4

Status Quo liked shopping when the weather was good—certain

legendary boutiques. Status Quo did not like shopping in the rain. She did not like sleet or any kind of very tiny, even, hurricane. She didn't like to sweat, either, except if perspiration was called for as it obviously was when she was on the treadmill with her headband on.

5

Status Quo had a nightmare. It could have been lurid. It might have involved her car! There might be a scratch on something right now—a rub, a nick, a cut, a scrape, a scuff. Status Quo said to nobody in particular that it was too dark to see.

6

Status Quo dipped her head in a bowl of lemons so as to attempt to alleviate the darkening. She would have tried peroxide but feared the slutty yellow. Status Quo ironed her pencil skirt. She decided to apply for a job at "Quarter till Eight," which she hoped was not a bar or a café, but a bank. She shook her one good pen two times. Three. Four. The heart of Status Quo was shaking then, like a real quake.

Cult Status

Cult Status were fluid, is how they would put it. Almost like rivulets. They went this way. They went that. They flowed, they wanted to say. They were a gush. They were a surge, to be honest, or a tide, especially first thing in the morning when they were first awake at the fridge, and they saw the bulb light up the hand almost like a moon before it reached the juice. That tiny instant before they grabbed the beverage and poured and drank it was for them almost a flood, really, of the them-ness and the they-ness that they carried so perfectly inside themselves like a flowering plant in their brains or loins or whatever until unfortunately for them they were forced to grasp that they were actually also a mishap if not a disaster, since the mother was the mother and the father, the father. And the banks, they were the banks. And the luck? It was the luck. Then the imperialism of the rest of the day would start loping after them like a migraine. What would a coma be like, they would want to ask someone. But nobody would be there.

Low Status

Was Low Status schizoid? Diabetic? Scaly? Obese? Did she drive some kind of speckled truck? A scooter? A horse? Was Low Status just ignorant? Had she no sense? Did she drink brandy? Did she eat okra? Was she from Germany? Puerto Rico? Charleston? Iraq? Was Low Status Black? Was her hair too puffy? Was it too flat? Did Low Status not shop? Where were her shoes? Why were they white? Was that her at McDonald's drinking a Coke? Is Low Status Delta Dawn? Is her heart broke? Is Low Status the short manager of a low-rent hotel? Is she a whore? Is that a paper clip in her ear? Is it a staple? Does Low Status pierce herself too much? Too obviously? Too wide? Is that dye in her hair? Does Low Status not travel overseas? Has she never seen a Renoir? A windbreaker? A pear?

PANTY STATUS

1

One Panty Status was too poor for underpants.

2

Two Panty Status would want *lingerie* or *thong* here so certain expectant scouts would do the equivalent of clap.

3

Certain heterosexuals, anyway, with a certain amount of verbal knack.

4

That's because Two Panty Status wanted this brief account to be for the people in their barns overlooking the pasture or the meadow if not the grassland per se.

5

Even *bra* would do it. Even *underthing*.

6

But *knickers?*

7

Britches?

8

Skivvies?

9

Two Panty Status didn't think so. She sat in her armchair by the window and thought *latex, really, people? Sock?*

10

Three Panty Status wanted to find a way to totally upend the American system of going to college to learn how to write PDFs and do PowerPoints and then or thereafter putting on a baseball cap or maybe a big straw garden hat until here's a lawn chair in a backyard of the suburbs outside Baltimore and here's a Honda or an Audi and therefore not a *casserole* so much as a *pot* to put gruel in and Goldilocks unfortunately therefore in her jammies and her muumuus.

11

Goldilocks in her onesies!

12

Her jammies!

13

Her muumuus!

SOCIAL STATUS

Social Status was Nobody's sister. Like Hansel and Gretel, they shared a poor father, a woodsy fireman. Their mother was dead and gone— infirmity, frailty, catastrophe, catastrophe. Social Status was a girl and Nobody was a boy. They lived in a little shanty in the mountains by a creek poisoned by Dow Chemical and fought incessantly on account of having such limited parental input.

Nobody once took Social Status's eyeliner and put it in the back of his truck to trick his girlfriend into thinking he was cheating on her. This was when Nobody was fifteen. Nobody had worked for two years selling skinned rabbits to buy his Ford. Social Status feared Nobody had taken her panties too and her best silk bra and several tampon applicators, but Social Status had no proof.

Nobody's main goal in life was to make a PDF pie chart of their father's frustration and to have a well-attended unveiling in the little village theater downtown. Social Status's goal in life was to leave Nobody far behind, but she kept a little notebook of everything Nobody put in *his* notebook anyway and knows therefore the extent to which she herself is no angel but, rather, a typhoon of want like a whole dug up Texas of it.

And that's what this is unfortunately about.

This is unfortunately about Social Status's need to be more among the few and more among the many.

This is not at all about Nobody.

Think of Social Status and then of Manhattan plus a London plus an Egypt. Think industrial park. Think the Atlantic, think the Pacific. Think under the Indian Ocean with that plane from Malaysia and all the volcanoes in Hawaii and anywhere else volcanoes go batty. Please think about all that lava inside the heart of poor Social Status in her wretched shanty.

STATUS GLAM

Status Glam wanted to be the Regis and Kathie Lee of Glam. She wanted to be the Liberace of Glam as in the Glam of Glam as she went from A to B on planes and boats and other conduits across everywhere spreading her Glam out to try to prevent it from becoming gaudy like the deep inside of the cunt of the corpse of a troll.

Status Glam was, in other words, a glitter slut who'd fuck any buck-eyed rat.

And she knew that. She plowed it.

She *farmed* it.

She spit on it and rubbed it to till it.

And wanted every American from California east and Texas north and Boston west and Michigan south to understand it too and knew they would if they could just start paying more attention and being more forgiving and just accept Status Glam for who Status Glam was because Status Glam really *needed* her own Glam-iness to please become more visible since desire like duplicity is also a hardship like a perfume that gusts and spreads because even though Status Glam knew she was the slick underside of the tongue of a frog, she didn't care because she just wanted the Glam so much her pretty little head hurt.

A *lot.*

But time is time. Time really *is* time.

Time's an old dog on a baked porch on a mountain of fog under such a sunny sun.

Regular Status Anxiety

Regular Status Anxiety was addicted to HGTV. Especially the bulldozers. Even just the thought of them. A PDF of a long list of the various names of them! She liked granite and pillows and refrigerators all smooth and built in and dogs that could fit in a homeowner's front pocket right before they got filmed flying off to Hawaii to be a con refugee. She liked real estate agents and architects and interior designers. She liked how everyone would work so faultlessly together to rip this asunder and then rip that.

The Tupperware, for example. The CorningWare. The barstools and the Walmart posters and the Kmart.

It all needed to just go.

The dirtied couch. The slotted spoon. The PC and the cell. The car, the truck, the boat, the Jeep.

Regular Status Anxiety also wanted a little reconstructive surgery. She wanted everything to just not rot. She wanted to suck on basil dipped in the oil of olive trees, but all alone somewhere like, say, a closet. She wanted not to think of the word *bye* followed by the word *bye* when she saw swallows and bats and lions and monkeys most especially at the zoo. And frogs of course and snakes and goats. She wanted to think of chickens also not at all.

Regular Status Anxiety wanted to think of chickens not ever.

Not their feathers not their bones not their juicy juice not once!

Regular Status Anxiety wanted to visit New York, but with more money than existed on the planet because otherwise no way. More money than God. A jet airliner filled to the neck in money. A money boat like a yacht only bigger like a Mars or a Saturn of money.

Which she'd fuck anybody for.

And swallow and blow.

And on and on toward complete invisibility.

By which we mean a pretty grave on a pretty hillside with pretty roses all laid out on the pretty ground like a pretty path somewhere in the pre-nuked spotlessness of, say, pre-nuked Japan.

Southern Status Anxiety

Southern Status Anxiety needed better bras. She needed stronger wire. She imagined herself standing in front of a big mirror in, say, Macy's downtown seeing how superior the uplift could be. Southern Status Anxiety also needed more mascara or better mascara like mascara made with maybe eucalyptus oil and charcoal or ground onyx or whatever—Southern Status Anxiety didn't exactly know how the mascara makers made their mascara and did not actually care since mostly she just needed someone such as a surgeon to staple the loose skin on her face to the back of her neck and the top of her skull. Southern Status Anxiety needed therefore a hat, if not a wig! It needed to be made of linen, for Southern Status Anxiety was hot. She was panting. She was tanning and panting. She was hot and tanning and pretty much literally burning to death on her deck while needing also a better bathing suit and more cellulose in her gut to avert the hunger until such time as a husband could be located out there in the galaxy where bad news seemed to whirl and eddy to such an awful extent that Southern Status Anxiety just needed a man and a deer he'd shoot or a rabid hog because what she was really needing right about now was a kill. And a cocktail party with lots and lots of vodka and bourbon and drink umbrellas and gin. And a swimming pool to go sit by and French sauvignon blanc and a fur for later when it would become winter and there would be a snowstorm and a Christmas tree would be necessary not to even mention the various wreaths and extra-large Jesus globes to hang from the windows with Jesus's handsome white

Jesus face and his even more handsome white Jesus sadness and white Jesus penis under the robes that she would never see because God, after all, was God.

Northern Status Anxiety

Peed once with X in a dull alley. Just a little dripping chat about the weather. Knew Y some too. Just a trifling lobby exchange, but still. Was on a panel with Z. But was already with T. Oh, and slept with A and B and told C once she had salmonella. Or was it E. coli? Drunk maybe. Off her ass. And was once on a flight with D. Stared for three hours at the back of that little woman's creepy neck. Dated the boyfriend also of E, who was nowhere near as important as A and B and even C, so why did she want to touch her blithely on the cheek in a cathedral where there'd be tents for some reason and flashlights and lamps and matches and Bics?

ACADEMIC STATUS ANXIETY

Academic Status Anxiety went to Yale. She went to Harvard. She went to Cambridge, she went to Oxford, she went to Swarthmore and to Stanford and to Berkeley where she laid down one day spontaneously on the tracks. She wanted a train to come. Just something to happen. She wanted to jump up just in time like she was all wings or air or light or song to sing the "Ode to Joy" to the mice and the foxes and the chickadees and the robins and the wrens. But Academic Status Anxiety went to the library instead. She took a test. And *there* she built her little nest.

OVERALL STATUS

Overall Status was the dull little roar of a person. You might even call her Zero Float. She didn't carp or whine. She did not drink. She didn't sing. She went to bed before Lawrence O'Donnell and did not ever sing or drink thanks to the Children's Choir at her house way back in 1968 all got all up in the loud but chaste finery of the ragbag dross of the faux fur required of them by the fashion rules of it being Christmas in America in 1968.

There was also lots of forest green, she remembered and guessed you called it, and blood red or whatever. And there was snow. It had been snowing all day long that day.

Her father was sleeping in his recliner behind her and did not wake when the choir's bells outside the front door began to ring. There were little bits of beer slobber on his collar. And there was Lawrence Welk on the TV with the volume off—she could see his piano out of the corner of her child-eye. Or was that Liberace?

Her father's sleeping hands rested on his sleeping thing below the bulbous belly. They held it, making a tent masking it that escalated it.

The Children's Choir said something about the faithful and sang ye and ye.

Overall Status shivered then and shut the savage door.

Not / a Spider in the Corner of a Jail / in the Middle of the Sahara in Late / July

ACADEMICIAN ABECEDARIAN STATUS

I am going to Boca Raton. & then it'll be off
to the Caribbean. Yes for a little rest & to selfie myself

reading Derrida but not Erasmus & not Ford Madox Ford
but just because I want God to eye me being me

as this is the hot-but-photographable twenty-first century
& because there's no islander Jesuit to stop me

plus no kerchief-wearing menace of a nimrod
oaf-picketing me either for being the queen of a rogue sham

straddling traveling like traveling's the dodge
I mean the uptick I mean the scheme the plot the ploy

& not the very best 1 percent way to dent
not so much the sad vagaries of what people call Being

as the pitiful yellow whatsits of the X of my Yankee lack of zeal
for living upfront I guess & fervent & nervy & still.

Coping Status

Here in the downward side
    of what's going on—
        in the blue hum

& airsick glum of it—
    I'm not dead yet
        & there's sauvignon blanc

in the fridge
    & an old shot glass & no shotgun
        & it's more or less nightfall

& there's an okay bed & a good pen
    & yeah I like my ink dark
        as dark gunmen

here in the downward side
    of what's going on
        where there are sawflies

& wild rye in a cauldron
    & the wings & bones
        of brown creepers & wrens

here near Massachusetts
    where I came to make my home
        to smell the ghosts of doomed women

in my cunt I want to say
    though that would be illogical
        & quite melodramatic

& unholy actually to the people of the hills
    where I'm from
        where the ladies make pies

on a weekly basis & bathe in creek waters
    & kiss you in your truck
        while they read ten thousand books

to get smart enough to arrive here
    to the downward side
        of what's going on

somewhere in the woods near Massachusetts
    all flimsy & woeful
        & woozy & broke.

Naysayer Status

Yes we are against our divorcing selves
& ourselves who feel so blest to be divorcing
& ourselves who like ourselves best without
our kids. & yes we are against our fat cells
& ourselves who are against our fat cells
though fat itself on pigs & cows we do admit
we are against if they're in a child's wagon
on Oprah on that episode we heard most upsets
the Oprah that Oprah & ourselves are against.
It's really just the money that Oprah & I
are against. Yes Oprah & I are against money
because we are against the selves in ourselves
who want the dopey things that money can buy
such as charcoal towels to dry off on the look
if not the feel of slate dipped in a gothic sensibility
exactly unlike something Oprah would give
Ma from that show *Little House on the Prairie*
there in her TV studio on earth in America
in Illinois in the big city of the many guns
that Oprah & I are so totally against. Yes
Oprah & I are against those who are against
our right to confess that we were wrong about
who to marry & what never to eat now that
we know so much about heart drought if not

how to say without people being against us
how much we love thimbles & teapots
& howling pink roses in the rain.

LIMBO STATUS

Mary Magdalene was a saint &
a disciple of Jesus & not my mom.
Unlike Mary Oliver & Mary Ruefle
& all the other Mary poets & other
just basic Mary people, Mary M
didn't write because she couldn't
even read—remember? & also never
drove a car or cursed a cop or bought
a mourning ring. Mary M never made
a single fucking thing with acetylene
or fell down face-first walking upstairs
or smoked a cig or got pushed in a park
on a broken silver swing. Mary M
some even depict as a whore! She was
from beside the Sea of Galilee & still
gets confused with Mary of Bethany
but here thanks to the laws of poetry
can & does signify every last thing
I don't know how to say about my mom
being atomized in the crematorium
after dying about a month or so ago
& so could be this wren at my window
or this wind that keeps me in this weird
Mary limbo or this weird song itself

linking "window" to "limbo," for my Mama|
liked songs & is anyway everywhere inside
my body—her cells & her proteins—her
hands & her feet—her lips—her knees—
     her wings—her wings—

Mental Health Status

Mama had died, so I
could toss my brief-
case & undo the latch
that did but did not
hinder my mouth.
I could go on & say
what a real in-dwell
of a hellish ground-
swell it was, the American
South. Yeah & divest
of my textiles in a
cafeteria or graveyard
or courthouse or council
chamber & stay un-
tethered this time for-
ever & oh & really
step into that space
between the fore
& the aft as in
really just love it
       once I have
swallowed the silver
& eaten of & in a bed
of kelp. Oh & arrived

ragged at Mama's
where she'd still be
faraway forever
& so said "seminal"
& meant it. Oh &
licked a hairbrush
of raw umber &
then just went on &
chewed it or burned it
& just went on & did
whatever & then some
to make a ravishing
catastrophe of my mother-
less self in this new
otherworld of zonk
& blow where all *them*
what's going goes.

Dead Mother Status

Little by little we gave up the hope of ever being
understood, Mary made her mouth wide
as a howl to confess. All I had to add to that
little piece of actuality was the question of
what to do now that my mother was dead.
I could forage for mushrooms since here it was
March again & spring had raced back home
with her hem so high & pink. I could go on
& put my arid head into this or that marshy
sink. Oh & ask Mary what else she'd lost
besides time & muscle definition & the bounce
of her luscious hair on the moonlit sheets.
Oh & perchance ask Mary if I could maybe
smack Mary for being alive now that my mother
was dead. Towering mother of the Titian hair
who'd been so forever-there. Towering mother
of the gift of such a peerless wit. & yet
Mama's hair was not in the end really Titian,
& everyone knows how much she resented it.
That so much of what's made can be by degrees
so altogether unmade is a terrible thing
to have to accept, & yet you *are* going
to have to learn to live with it, Mary.
In both the dictionary & in the thesaurus,

Mary. In the kitchen! In the car! In the forest
plucking mushrooms from the base
of the soggy trunks of the umpteen aspen trees
& tossing them into the craven center
of your motherless mouth! With that
killer wind just yowling. With it not.

MOURNING STATUS

Mary too could be the bones of lost water
in black water or just basic river water
drunk on even more water up in the hills
in a sluice of water made of my mother's ashes
like there's such a thing as a glut of water
made of water & you can call it Mary if you
want to. We all took a handful of my mother
& spread her out under the old maples
before & after it rained & there she sits without
her legs like a cello I thought until I felt her
flatten out under the water & spread like a moth
among the moths or a bat among the bats
or a moth inside the belly of a bat I will call Mary
if you don't mind since Mary is the name
for everything my mother has become
out there without me like a cloudburst of bluebells
I would say if I could believe it or if you could
or if the world were right & bluebells could rain.

STATUS REPORT

I love-love-*loved* the alphabet
back when I could use it to go OMG & WTF

vis-à-vis some shady late-capitalist wrongdoing
such as the rich & famous floating off the continent

in the most flagrant of boats, leaving just
the youngsters & me here on the prairie

to keep everything intact with just this sugar on the mantle
in its charismatic tin. But then the youngsters

got up from the knitting circle & put down their seedcakes
& other organic whatsits, saying OMG & WTF to me

as in *in reference to me* like what I had on was not just
the dress, the feeling unfortunately was, but also

a shawl as in a cloak as in a stole as in a shroud.
That's when I finally knew what animals youngsters

just naturally are. What piles of tractor parts.
What fish heads in a sink! So now I'm using my Rosetta stone

to examine the language of rhinos for the impenetrable skin
& the language of axes for the battle for when our foes return

to knock down our pretty little door. & here
I just wanted to sit out the rest of my days

with my sweeties by the hearth & talk the talk to hold at bay
whatever apocalyptic thing's got our number as in our address

as in the extent to which we were born to fight moneyed reprobates
with just our lingo as in our candidness & cheeky verbal fluidity

if that's what you want to call running out the clock on the ends of
    things
        in an old lonesome song like this.

PRIVATION STATUS

Not starving, not in chemo,
not yet inadmissibly crackpot.
Not shot up in a scrawny boat
at sea. Not kidnapped & slain
unhurriedly. Not mutilated
& martyred. Not hauled up
from the grave like S. Dali
for some little lawyer to prove
who I'm not the long-ago
unwitting parent of. Not
a spider in the corner of a jail
in middle of the Sahara in late
July. But woe anyway to me
in the new Dollar General
where the hayfield used to be
wanting tampons
with cardboard applicators
but finding just the pink & white
plastic ones. As though
there weren't a huge vortex
of trash in the Pacific. As though
my predicament weren't
ridiculous. O, great slimy
garbage patch of fork & knife

& water bottle & Chinese ukulele
& Bud ring & whatever
other unrotted whatnot
teeming salty now in one of
the great nitty-gritty seas of this
earth! If you're a wrong—&
you're worse than wrong—I'm
just as bad since I'm theoretically
at least alive here in a yellow aisle
of mislaid whippoorwills & mice
& voles they say used to live
in the hayfield & kestrels & butterflies
& foxes & rabbits & June bugs
& not any kind of fish of course
but grasshopper they say used
to live in the aisle here & possum
& groundhog & swallow & bat.

♥

Fox Heart

          There is no La Leche League
in the Appalachian rainforest in my heart. There is
no Gap, no Eileen Fisher, no Wi-Fi, no Dollar General.
But for 500 million years at least there was
enough chestnut & littleleaf sneezeweed & Carolina parakeet
for everybody in the Appalachian rainforest in my heart
& in actual reality plus megatons of satiny swarms
of freshwater mussels the pearly shells of which
make good ashtrays & southern bog lemming
& woodland bison & elk—*elk!*—plus actual
passenger pigeons & certain kinds of big-eared bats
& shrews. But the freshwater mussels these days
like the wild leek & the mountain alder & the piratebush
are turning to an invisible blur in the old rivers

                    of the Appalachian rainforest
in my heart & in actual reality not to even mention
the shrimp-like crayfish they'd dare us to swallow live at 4-H
to prove what hillbillies we were & how much we loved
the forest & everything already dead & dying in it.
So of course I stood there on stage in that hunting lodge
& shut my eyes to imagine the gray fox also in my heart
& in reality as the fox is one of the high priests of all this listing
by which I just mean the main gumption behind it

mostly because she's still flourishing in her sly den
with the scattered bones like a fence line outside
since she's too busy not to be messy & far too hungry
not to sleep all day & hunt all night & too maternal
& sneaky not to steal chickens for her kits

        & too curious not to stare at everything forever
to discern it. The gray fox can even climb trees & is hence
also part coon & cat & I do mourn the mountain lion—
I remember as a child the bobcat's call—& I do mourn
never seeing a flying squirrel or a star-nosed mole
or a bog turtle or a diamond darter or a spruce-fir moss spider
& hate not even knowing what a hellbender is, but still
I stood there on stage in that 4-H hunting lodge
in my beloved Blue Ridge at the age of eight & shut my eyes
to call up the grey fox hiding out in a little den in the shadow
of my hillbilly heart to get the guts to open my mouth
& swallow that crayfish live so I could learn I think
to bide my time till I could sing this story of our unforgiveable sins
& try & say what a fierce little forever-thing at least our sorrow is.

NOTES

Someone I didn't recognize on CNN and thus can't name here spoke the first two and thereafter repeating lines of "Coping Status" ("Here in the downward side of what's going on") during the late spring days of 2020, when the scope of the seriousness of the COVID-19 pandemic was just becoming clear.

The Elizabeth Strout quote opening this book is taken from her book *Lucy by the Sea* (Random House, 2022).

The first line of "Status, Alas" is taken from a chapter in Mathew Klam's *Who Is Rich?* (Random House, 2017).

As the speaker says he does in "Fallout Status," A.R. Ammons does ask in *Garbage* if *Garbage* "can't be if…not the best poem of the / century, …about the worst poem of the / century." *Garbage* won the National Book Award in 1993 (W.W. Norton, 1993).

The last line of "Mother May I Status" is borrowed from William Gay's *Twilight* (Dzanc Books, 2015).

The first line of "Dead Mother Status" begins with lines borrowed from Mary Ruefle's poem "The Estate of Single Blessedness" (from *Trances of the Blast*, Wave Books, 2013), and is after her, as we are wont to say, and for her.

"Status Report" was first published in *Appalachians Run Amok* (Two Sylvias Press, 2018), and is included here to keep the status sequence intact.

ACKNOWLEDGMENTS

Deepest thanks to the editors who first published many of the poems in this collection, most in earlier versions and a few with titles that were later used for different poems as my understanding of the sequence grew. May the record here keep any future archivists content, if not quite happy.

American Poetry Review, Briar Cliff Review, Chattahoochee Review, Connotation Press, Crazyhorse, Diode, Florida Review, Jung Journal, Louisville Review, Meat for Tea, Mudfish, Ninth Letter, Ocean State Review, Phantom Drift, Pleiades, RHINO, Shenandoah, Storyscape, Washington Square Review, Waxwing.

"Fox Heart" was commissioned by and first published in *Literary Field Guide to Southern Appalachia*, Georgia University Press, 2019.

"Bereavement Status" was first published in *Wait: Poems from the Pandemic*, edited by Jeri Theriault, Littoral Books, 2001.

Thanks to Colby College for the sabbatical without which this book would not exist.

Forever love and thanks to Colin Cheney, Lynn Emanuel, Lisa Lewis, Cate Marvin, Jefferson Navicky, and Ira Sadoff for tolerating these poems at their roughest and giving me the strength not to give up on the whole project many times over. Forever love and thanks to Rodney Jones for also having faith in this book before I could come anywhere close to mustering it. Forever love and thanks to Cedric Bryant for saving me in ways that cannot be articulated in this sentence but I hope will be in other books down the road. Forever love and thanks to Martha Rhodes for seeing whatever virtues are here, and for being so patient with my fears and worries. Thanks to Ryan Murphy and the whole team at Four Way Books for keeping me on the straight and narrow during the production process. And Nancy Koerbel and Mary Lewis: so so *so* many thanks! I would be truly lost without each and every one of you.

Adrian Blevins is the author of three previous full-length collections of poetry—*Appalachians Run Amok*, *Live from the Homesick Jamboree*, and *The Brass Girl Brouhaha*—and, with co-editor Karen Salyer McElmurray, *Walk Till the Dogs Get Mean*, a collection of essays by new and emerging Appalachian writers. She is the recipient of many awards and honors including the Wilder Prize from Two Sylvias Press, a Kate Tufts Discovery Award, and a Rona Jaffe Writer's Foundation Award. She is a professor of English at Colby College in Waterville, Maine, where she directs the Creative Writing Program.

PUBLICATION OF THIS BOOK WAS MADE POSSIBLE
BY GRANTS AND DONATIONS.

WE ARE ALSO GRATEFUL TO THOSE INDIVIDUALS WHO PARTICIPATED IN OUR BUILD A BOOK PROGRAM. THEY ARE:

Anonymous (14), Robert Abrams, Michael Ansara, Kathy Aponick, Michael Anna de Armas, Jean Ball, Sally Ball, Clayre Benzadón, Adrian Blevins, Laurel Blossom, Adam Bohannon, Betsy Bonner, Patricia Bottomley, Lee Briccetti, Joel Brouwer, Susan Buttenwieser, Anthony Cappo, Paul and Brandy Carlson, Dan Clarke, Mark Conway, Elinor Cramer, Kwame Dawes, John Del Peschio, Brian Komei Dempster, Patrick Donnelly, Lynn Emanuel, Blas Falconer, Jennifer Franklin, John Gallaher, Reginald Gibbons, Rebecca Kaiser Gibson, Dorothy Tapper Goldman, Julia Guez, Naomi Guttman and Jonathan Mead, Forrest Hamer, Luke Hankins, Yona Harvey, KT Herr, Karen Hildebrand, Carlie Hoffman, Glenna Horton, Thomas and Autumn Howard, Catherine Hoyser, Elizabeth Jackson, Linda Susan Jackson, Jessica Jacobs and Nickole Brown, Lee Jenkins, Elizabeth Kanell, Nancy Kassell, Maeve Kinkead, Victoria Korth, Brett Lauer and Gretchen Scott, Howard Levy, Owen Lewis and Susan Ennis, Margaree Little, Sara London and Dean Albarelli, Tariq Luthun, Myra Malkin, Louise Mathias, Victoria McCoy, Lupe Mendez, Michael and Nancy Murphy, Kimberly Nunes, Susan Okie and Walter Weiss, Cathy McArthur Palermo, Veronica Patterson, Jill Pearlman, Marcia and Chris Pelletiere, Sam Perkins, Susan Peters and Morgan Driscoll, Maya Pindyck, Megan Pinto, Kevin Prufer, Martha Rhodes and Jean Brunel, Paula Rhodes, Louise Riemer, Peter and Jill Schireson, Rob Schlegel, Yoana Setzer, Soraya Shalforoosh, Mary Slechta, Diane Souvaine, Barbara Spark, Catherine Stearns, Jacob Strautmann, Yerra Sugarman, Arthur Sze and Carol Moldaw, Marjorie and Lew Tesser, Dorothy Thomas, Rosalynde Vas Dias, Rushi Vyas, Martha Webster and Robert Fuentes, Abby Wender and Rohan Weerasinghe, Rachel Weintraub and Allston James, and Monica Youn.